The Financial Freedom **Work** → Book

Edward Mitchell Jones

For permission requests, write to the author at the address below.
Dr.Jones@ExpandedEducationalServices.com and or
Memphis, Tennessee 38141

This book was edited, formatted, designed, and published by:
UNIQUE PUBLISHING HOUSE, LLC
P.O. Box 750792, Memphis, TN 38175
www.uniquehouse.org

ISBN: 978-1-971885-00-1

The Financial Freedom **Work** → Book

Edward Mitchell Jones

DEDICATION

To my lovely wife, Dr. Candace Jones.

To the students of Rescue Enterprise, this will help you as you work your way into financial freedom.

To all of the students of EES Success Academy, this material is for you as well! You won't struggle with this later in life because you were trained in your youth. You will be teaching others, because you've prepared yourself to be the head – not the tail!

TABLE OF CONTENTS

WORKBOOK INTRODUCTION

Welcome to the Financial Freedom Action Workbook. This workbook is designed to help you take real steps toward getting your money under control. The exercises in these pages will help you understand your habits, see where your money is going, build better routines, and make clear decisions that bring peace and stability to your life.

Go at your own pace, but stay consistent. Work through one page at a time. Be honest. Write everything down — even the things you don't want to see. The goal is progress, not perfection. Small steps done over and over again lead to big change.

Use this workbook daily, weekly, or as often as you need. The more you use it, the stronger you become in handling your money.

I am excited to walk with you into your financial freedom. Let's get started!

Edward M. Jones

HOW TO USE THIS WORKBOOK

This workbook is designed to help you take the principles in the *Financial Victory* book and turn them into real habits that change your life. The goal here isn't to rush or impress anybody — it's to be honest, consistent, and focused. Each section helps you see your money clearly, make better choices, and build discipline step by step.

You'll write things down, track what you spend, and plan ahead instead of reacting. Don't skip pages, don't guess, and don't rush. Take your time. Be real with yourself. The more honest you are on paper, the faster your money will change in real life.

Use this workbook daily or at least several times a week. Keep it with you. Bring it to your sessions with Edward. Write in it when a thought hits you. This book becomes a record of your progress.

SETTING YOUR MIND FOR CHANGE

Changing your money starts with changing the way you think. Before you improve your finances, you have to decide you're ready to do things differently. This means slowing down, paying attention, and choosing habits that support your goals instead of fighting against them.

You may be used to swiping, eating out, moving fast, or spending without thinking — but now you're learning a new way. Some days will feel easy, some will feel uncomfortable. That's normal. Stay committed. Remind yourself why you're doing this: for peace, stability, freedom, better sleep, and a better future.

Your results won't come from big, dramatic moves. They'll come from small, smart decisions repeated over time. That's how you build real financial victory.

YOUR 90-DAY COMMITMENT

For the next 90 days, you're making a personal commitment to follow the Financial Victory steps without quitting. This is your time to get serious, build discipline, and prove to yourself that change is possible.

Here is your commitment for the next 90 days:

- I will track my spending honestly.
- I will use cash instead of swiping whenever possible.
- I will cook more meals at home and limit eating out.
- I will work my side hustle and save the money I earn.
- I will focus on paying off my smallest debts first.
- I will read my money goals weekly to stay focused.
- I will not give up when it gets uncomfortable.

At the end of these 90 days, you will be in a better position than when you started — financially, mentally, and emotionally. This commitment is not to impress Edward or anyone else. It is a promise you are making to your future self.

SECTION 1 — KNOWING WHERE YOU STAND

This section helps you understand your current financial habits, your thinking, and your real numbers. Before anything can change, you need to see the truth clearly.

1.1 — MONEY MINDSET CHECK-IN

INSTRUCTIONS:

Answer the questions honestly. There is no right or wrong answer. This is just to understand where you are mentally with money.

Reflection Questions

1. When I think about money, I usually feel:
   - ☐ Calm
   - ☐ Stressed
   - ☐ Confused
   - ☐ Hopeful
   - ☐ Tired
   - ☐ Other: ______________________

2. The first word that comes to mind when I hear "budget" is:

   ____

3. Growing up, I learned that money was:

   ____

4. My biggest fear about money is:

   ____

5. I wish I could change this one money habit right now:

   ____

6. One thing I want money to help me do this year is:

   ____

MINDSET SUMMARY

Write one short paragraph about what you discovered about the way you think about money:

1.2 — YOUR INCOME SNAPSHOT

INSTRUCTIONS: List every source of income you currently have. If income changes month to month, write the average.

Income Source	Amount Per Month	Notes
Job	$	
Side hustle	$	
Child support	$	
Assistance	$	
Other	$	
TOTAL MONTHLY INCOME	**$**	

Irregular Income Worksheet

If your income changes:

- Write the highest amount you make: $____________
- Write the lowest amount you make: $____________
- Write the safe amount to budget with: $____________

This helps prevent panic during slow months.

1.3 — YOUR EXPENSE SNAPSHOT

Fixed Expenses (same every month). Examples: rent, phone, insurance.

Expense	**Amount**	**Notes**
____________________	$	
____________________	$	
____________________	$	
TOTAL FIXED EXPENSES:	**$**	

VARIABLE EXPENSES (change every month)

Examples: food, gas, eating out, shopping.

Expense	**Amount**	**Notes**
Food (Groceries)	$________	
Gas	$________	
Eating out	$________	
Miscellaneous	$________	
TOTAL VARIABLE EXPENSES:	**$________**	

Total Monthly Expenses:

Fixed + Variable = **$**__________

1.4 — 7-DAY SPENDING TRACKER

INSTRUCTIONS: For the next 7 days, write down **every single purchase**, no matter how small. If you spend it, **write it**.

Day	What You Spent Money On	Amount	Cash or Card?
Monday	______________________________	$______	☐ Cash ☐ Card
Tuesday	______________________________	$______	☐ Cash ☐ Card
Wednesday	___________________________	$______	☐ Cash ☐ Card
Thursday	____________________________	$______	☐ Cash ☐ Card
Friday	_______________________________	$______	☐ Cash ☐ Card
Saturday	____________________________	$______	☐ Cash ☐ Card
Sunday	_______________________________	$______	☐ Cash ☐ Card

7-DAY REFLECTION

1. What surprised you the most?

2. Did you swipe more than you expected?

3. Did you eat out more than you thought?

4. Where do you see money slipping away?

1.5 — "WHERE IS MY MONEY GOING?" SUMMARY PAGE

Total Spent on Eating Out This Week: $__________

Total Spent on Groceries: $__________

Total Swiped on Card: $__________

Total Spent in Cash: $__________

What I Learned:

Write one short paragraph about what this week taught you.

SECTION 1 NOTES

SECTION 2 — BUILDING BETTER HABITS

These habits are the backbone of financial Freedom. They are simple, practical, and easy to follow — but they must be done *on purpose.* This section helps you build strong routines that keep more money in your pocket.

2.1 — THE NO-SWIPE CHALLENGE

INSTRUCTIONS: For the next 7 or 30 days, do not swipe your debit card or credit card unless it's an emergency. Use cash only for daily spending. Swiping is one of the fastest ways to lose track of your money. Cash keeps you honest.

Choose your challenge: ☐ 7-Day No-Swipe ☐ 30-Day No-Swipe

DAILY NO-SWIPE CHALLENGE TRACKER

Day	**Did I Swipe? (Yes/No)**	**What Happened Today?**	**Notes**
Day 1	☐ Yes ☐ No		
Day 2	☐ Yes ☐ No		
Day 3	☐ Yes ☐ No		
Day 4	☐ Yes ☐ No		
Day 5	☐ Yes ☐ No		
Day 6	☐ Yes ☐ No		
Day 7	☐ Yes ☐ No		
Day 8–30 (if chosen)			

REFLECTION

1. When did you most feel tempted to swipe?

2. What helped you stay disciplined?

3. How did using cash change your thinking?

2.2 — THE EAT-IN CHALLENGE

Eating in is one of the biggest money savers — and most people underestimate how much they spend eating out.

INSTRUCTIONS: Choose to cook all meals at home for:

☐ 3 days

☐ 7 days

☐ 14 days

☐ A full month

MEAL PLANNING SHEET

Breakfast Ideas:

Lunch Ideas:

Dinner Ideas:

Snacks:

GROCERY LIST TEMPLATE

Item	Qty	Cost	Notes
____________________	______	$______	______
____________________	______	$______	______
____________________	______	$______	______
____________________	______	$______	______
____________________	______	$______	______
____________________	______	$______	______
____________________	______	$______	______
____________________	______	$______	______
____________________	______	$______	______

Estimated Grocery Total: $__________

COST COMPARISON

What I usually spend eating out in one week:

BREAKFAST $__________ LUNCH $__________ DINNER $__________

SNACKS/TREATS

$__________ $__________ $__________ $__________

What I spent on groceries for the Eat-In Challenge: $__________

Money saved: $__________

REFLECTION

1. How did eating at home help you financially?

2. What meals were easiest? Hardest?

3. Will you continue eating in more often? Why or why not?

2.3 — CASH-ONLY WEEK

Cash *makes* you think. Swiping does not.

INSTRUCTIONS: Take out one week's spending money in cash. Use ONLY that cash for the entire week.

Recommended weekly amounts:	Put your cash in labeled envelopes:
☐ $40 ☐ $60 ☐ $80 ☐ Other: $__________	• Groceries • Gas • Personal Spending • Household Items

ENVELOPE TRACKER

Envelope	Starting Cash	What You Spent	Ending Cash
Groceries	$______	$______	$______
Gas	$______	$______	$______
Personal	$______	$______	$______
Household	$______	$______	$______

REFLECTION QUESTIONS

1. Did using cash change how you made decisions?

   ____

2. Did you run out early or finish with money left over?

   ____

3. Which envelope needs adjusting for next week?

   ____

2.4 — MANAGING YOUR OWN PAYMENTS

Automatic payments seem convenient, but they can wreck your account if timing is off.

INSTRUCTIONS: Use this sheet to list every bill you have. Then choose the exact day YOU plan to pay it.

Bill	Amount	Due Date	I Will Pay On	Method (Cash/App/Online)
____________	$______	______	______	______
____________	$______	______	______	______
____________	$______	______	______	______
____________	$______	______	______	______

LATE FEE PREVENTION PLAN

1. One thing I can do to avoid late fees:

____

2. Which bill needs more attention?

____

3. One reminder I will set (calendar, phone alarm, sticky note):

____

2.5 — BUILD YOUR HUSTLE PLAN

Your hustle gives you breathing room. It's your extra income, your backup plan, and your future opportunity.

INSTRUCTIONS: Use the sheets below to discover your skills and turn them into side income.

SKILLS INVENTORY

Write down **everything** you are good at — even small things.

- ____
- ____
- ____
- ____

HUSTLE IDEAS BRAINSTORM

Use your skills above to create possible hustle ideas.

- ____
- ____
- ____
- ____

PRICING WORKSHEET

Service / Product	What Others Charge	What I Will Charge	Notes
____________________	$______	$______	______
____________________	$______	$______	______
____________________	$______	$______	______

WEEKLY HUSTLE LOG

Day	What I Did	Hours	Money Earned
Monday	____________________	______	$______
Tuesday	____________________	______	$______
Wednesday	__________________	______	$______
Thursday	___________________	______	$______
Friday	_____________________	______	$______
Saturday	___________________	______	$______
Sunday	_____________________	______	$______

Weekly Total Earned: $__________

SECTION 2 NOTES

SECTION 3 — PAYING DOWN DEBT THE SMART WAY

Debt does not disappear by ignoring it. To get ahead, you must know exactly what you owe, choose the right debt to attack first, and follow a simple plan consistently. This section helps you do just that.

3.1 — KNOW YOUR DEBTS

INSTRUCTIONS: List EVERY debt you have — big or small.

This includes:

- credit cards ______________ ______________ ______________
- medical bills ______________ ______________ ______________
- loans ______________ ______________ ______________
- payday loans ______________ ______________ ______________
- personal loans ______________ ______________ ______________
- car payments ______________ ______________ ______________
- collections ______________ ______________ ______________

Do NOT skip anything.

DEBT OVERVIEW WORKSHEET

Creditor / Bill	Balance Owed	Minimum Payment	Interest Rate	Due Date
________________	$__________	$________	_______%	______
________________	$__________	$________	_______%	______
________________	$__________	$________	_______%	______
________________	$__________	$________	_______%	______
________________	$__________	$________	_______%	______

TOTAL DEBT: $_______________

TOTAL MONTHLY MINIMUM PAYMENTS: $________________

INTEREST REALITY CHECK

Answer the following:

1. Which debt has the highest interest rate?

2. Which debt has the smallest balance?

3. Which one stresses you out the most?

4. Which one feels easiest to pay off right now?

3.2 — PICK YOUR FIRST PAYOFF TARGET

The quickest way to build momentum is to *pay off the smallest debt first* — even if it's not the highest interest rate. A quick win builds confidence.

INSTRUCTIONS: Choose the smallest debt from your list.

MY FIRST TARGET DEBT

- Creditor: ___________________________________
- Balance: $___________________________________
- Minimum Payment: $___________________________
- Due Date: __________________________________

Now choose how much EXTRA you will pay each month:

- Extra amount: $__________________________

PAYOFF PLAN SHEET

Month	Minimum Payment	Extra Payment	New Balance	Notes
Month 1	$______	$______	$______	__________
Month 2	$______	$______	$______	__________
Month 3	$______	$______	$______	__________
Month 4	$______	$______	$______	__________
Month 5	$______	$______	$______	__________
Month 6	$______	$______	$______	__________

CHECK-IN QUESTIONS

1. Did paying extra feel possible this month?

____

2. What habits helped you stay on track?

____

3. What made it difficult?

____

3.3 — THE 30-DAY CREDIT CARD RULE

Credit cards are not evil — but interest will drain you. The rule is simple: *If you can't pay it off in 30 days, you don't need it.*

INSTRUCTIONS: Use this sheet to help you break the cycle.

CARD USE REFLECTION

1. How many cards do you have?

   ____

2. Are any maxed out?

   ☐ Yes

   ☐ No

3. Do you know what you bought with them?

   ☐ Yes

   ☐ No

   Notes: ______________________________

4. Which card is your lowest balance card?

   ____

CARD-FREE WEEK TRACKER

Day	Did I Use a Card? (Yes/No)	What Happened?
Monday	☐ Yes ☐ No	____________________
Tuesday	☐ Yes ☐ No	____________________
Wednesday	☐ Yes ☐ No	____________________
Thursday	☐ Yes ☐ No	____________________
Friday	☐ Yes ☐ No	____________________
Saturday	☐ Yes ☐ No	____________________
Sunday	☐ Yes ☐ No	____________________

Goal: Get through the entire week with NO card use!

3.4 — DEBT SNOWBALL OR SNOWFLAKE WORKSHEET

The *Snowball Method* helps you pay off the smallest debt first. The *Snowflake Method* uses small extra payments whenever you find extra cash. Both work — choose the one that fits you best.

MY SNOWBALL PLAN

List debts from smallest to largest:

Order	Debt Name	Balance	Payment
1	____________	$______	$______
2	____________	$______	$______
3	____________	$______	$______
4	____________	$______	$______
5	____________	$______	$______
6	____________	$______	$______

MONTHLY DEBT SNOWBALL TRACKER

Month	Debt Paid Off?	New Debt Target	Notes
Month 1	☐ Yes ☐ No	______________	__________
Month 2	☐ Yes ☐ No	______________	__________
Month 3	☐ Yes ☐ No	______________	__________
Month 4	☐ Yes ☐ No	______________	__________
Month 5	☐ Yes ☐ No	______________	__________
Month 6	☐ Yes ☐ No	______________	__________
Month 7	☐ Yes ☐ No	______________	__________
Month 8	☐ Yes ☐ No	______________	__________
Month 9	☐ Yes ☐ No	______________	__________

Month 10	☐ Yes ☐ No	____________________	___________
Month 11	☐ Yes ☐ No	____________________	___________
Month 12	☐ Yes ☐ No	____________________	___________

SNOWFLAKE LOG — SMALL EXTRA PAYMENTS

Write down every extra amount you put toward debt — even $1 counts.

Date	Amount	Where It Came From	New Balance
________	$______	______________________	$______
________	$______	______________________	$______
________	$______	______________________	$______
________	$______	______________________	$______
________	$______	______________________	$______
________	$______	______________________	$______
________	$______	______________________	$______
________	$______	______________________	$______
________	$______	______________________	$______

END-OF-SECTION REFLECTION

1. What did you learn about your debt?

2. Which debt do you feel confident about tackling next?

3. What small habit will help you stay on track?

SECTION 3 NOTES

SECTION 4 — SAVING WITH PURPOSE

Saving money is not about having a big paycheck — it's about having a clear plan. Even small amounts add up fast when you stay consistent. This section helps you build savings the simple way.

4.1 — YOUR FIRST SAVINGS GOAL

INSTRUCTIONS: Choose ONE goal to focus on first. Keeping it simple helps you win faster.

Common first goals:

- $500 emergency fund
- One month of groceries saved
- One insurance payment saved
- $1,000 in savings
- Car tags/registration
- Extra bill payment
- Car repair fund

MY FIRST SAVINGS GOAL

My goal is: ____

Amount Needed: $____

Deadline: ____

SAVINGS BREAKDOWN SHEET

How much do you need to save each:

Timeframe	**Amount**
Per month	$________________
Per week	$________________
Per day (optional)	$________________

This lets you know exactly what you're aiming for.

WHY THIS GOAL MATTERS

Write one short paragraph about why this goal is important to you:

4.2 — THE "SAVE WHAT YOU USED TO SPEND" PAGE

This page helps you save money by redirecting what you used to spend somewhere else.

INSTRUCTIONS: Pick a spending habit and convert the money into savings.

Ideas:

- Eating out
- Coffee runs
- Beauty/high-maintenance extras
- Delivery fees
- Fast food
- Daily snacks
- Impulse shopping

SPENDING REPLACEMENT WORKSHEET

Old Spending Habit	Weekly Amount	Monthly Savings if Replaced
____________________	$______	$______
____________________	$______	$______

CAR-PAYMENT SAVINGS TRACKER

A *Genius Jones, Millionaire Mindset & Financial Freedom* strategy. When a car (or another large bill) is almost paid off, SAVE the payment after it's paid — don't spend it!

Month	**Car Payment Saved**	**New Savings Total**	**Notes**
Month 1	$______	$______	__________
Month 2	$______	$______	__________
Month 3	$______	$______	__________
Month 4	$______	$______	__________
Month 5	$______	$______	__________
Month 6	$______	$______	__________
Month 7	$______	$______	__________
Month 8	$______	$______	__________

This is how you stay ahead of repairs, emergencies, and future trips WITHOUT stress.

CRUISE VS. CAR WORKSHEET

A *Genius Jones, Millionaire Mindset & Financial Freedom* signature teaching!

Cost of a cruise or vacation: $________________

What could be paid off instead?

If I skipped this cruise, how much could be saved or paid off?

Would skipping it help me more long-term?

☐ Yes

☐ No

4.3 — WEEKLY SAVINGS CHALLENGE

Choose a challenge that fits your income and life right now. Make several copies of this sheet so you can track this entire year.

OPTION A — $5 WEEKLY CHALLENGE

52 weeks x $5 = **$260 saved**

Week	Saved	Total
1 ________________	$5	$5
2 ________________	$5	$10
3 ________________	$5	$15
________________	$5	$____
________________	$5	$____
________________	$5	$____
________________	$5	$____

OPTION B — $10 WEEKLY CHALLENGE

52 weeks x $10 = **$520 saved**

Week	Saved	Total
1________________	$10	$10
2________________	$10	$20
3________________	$10	$30
4________________	$10	$____
5________________	$10	$____
6________________	$10	$____
7________________	$10	$____
8________________	$10	$____

OPTION C — $20 WEEKLY CHALLENGE

52 weeks x $20 = **$1,040 saved**

Week	**Saved**	**Total**
1________________	$20	$20
2________________	$20	$40
3________________	$20	$60
4________________	$20	$____
5________________	$20	$____
6________________	$20	$____
7________________	$20	$____
8________________	$20	$____

OPTION D — FLEXIBLE WEEKLY CHALLENGE

Save what you can each week: Make several copies of this sheet so you can track this entire year.

Week	Amount Saved	New Total	Notes
1	$______	$______	______
2	$______	$______	______
3	$______	$______	______
4	______	______	______
5	______	______	______
6	______	______	______
7	______	______	______
8	______	______	______

4.4 — FOOD SAVINGS TRACKER

Food spending is one of the biggest areas where money leaks. This tracker helps you compare eating out versus cooking at home.

EAT-IN SAVINGS LOG

Every time you skip eating out, write the money amount here:

Date	**What You Skipped**	**Amount Saved**
______	____________________	$______
______	____________________	$______
______	____________________	$______
______	____________________	$______
______	____________________	$______
______	____________________	$______

MONTHLY FOOD BUDGET WORKSHEET

Category	Budgeted	Actual	Difference
Groceries	$______	$______	+/- $______
Eating Out	$______	$______	+/- $______
Snacks/Coffee	$______	$______	+/- $______
Fast Food	$______	$______	+/- $______

FOOD EXPENSE REFLECTION

1. What surprised me most this month?

   ____

2. How much did I save by eating at home?

   ____

3. One change I will keep doing next month is:

   ____

SECTION 5 — YOUR 90-DAY MONEY PLAN

You don't have to change everything at once. But you *do* need a simple plan you can follow for the next 90 days. This section breaks your journey into three clear months, each with:

- Monthly goals
- Weekly actions
- Progress check-ins
- Reflection pages

By the end of 90 days, you'll see real changes in your habits, money, and confidence.

HOW THE 90-DAY PLAN WORKS

- Month 1: Awareness & Reset
  - ☐ You see the truth.
  - ☐ You track spending.
  - ☐ You stop swiping.
  - ☐ You reset your habits.
- Month 2: Discipline & Action
  - ☐ You follow the rules.
  - ☐ You eat in more.
  - ☐ You pay on your first debt.
  - ☐ You manage your own payments.
- Month 3: Growth & Consistency
  - ☐ You stay steady.
  - ☐ You save on purpose.
  - ☐ You build your hustle.
  - ☐ You keep gaining confidence.

MONTH 1 — AWARENESS & RESET

MONTH 1 GOALS

List 2–4 goals you want to accomplish this month.

1. ______________________________
2. ______________________________
3. ______________________________
4. ______________________________

WEEKLY ACTIONS FOR MONTH 1

(Do these each week.)

- ☐ Track every dollar spent
- ☐ Use cash instead of swiping
- ☐ Cook at home at least 3 days a week
- ☐ Review your bills
- ☐ Identify ONE habit to stop
- ☐ Check your bank account twice this week

WEEK 1 CHECK-IN

1. Something I did well:

2. Something I need to improve:

3. One thing I learned about my spending:

WEEK 2 CHECK-IN

1. Something I did well:

2. Something I need to improve:

3. One thing I learned about my spending:

WEEK 3 CHECK-IN

1. Something I did well:

2. Something I need to improve:

3. One thing I learned about my spending:

WEEK 4 CHECK-IN

1. Something I did well:

2. Something I need to improve:

3. One thing I learned about my spending:

MONTH 1 — END-OF-MONTH REFLECTION

1. Total saved this month: $____________
2. Total spent eating out: $____________
3. Total paid toward debt: $____________
4. Biggest habit that changed:
5. One thing I'm proud of:
6. One thing I will keep working on:

MONTH 2 — DISCIPLINE & ACTION

This is where things shift. This month you focus on discipline and steady routines.

MONTH 2 GOALS

1. ______________________________
2. ______________________________
3. ______________________________
4. ______________________________

WEEKLY ACTIONS FOR MONTH 2

- No-Swipe Challenge continues
- Eat-in Challenge continues
- Pay on your FIRST debt target
- Use cash envelopes
- Pay every bill yourself (no auto-pay)
- Track your hustle hours or earnings

WEEK 1 CHECK-IN

Use the same set of questions each week:

1. What worked well this week?
2. What did I struggle with?
3. Did I use cash more than my card?
4. Did I cook at home more than last month?
5. Did I make progress on my debt target?

WEEK 2 CHECK-IN

Use the same set of questions each week:

1. What worked well this week?
2. What did I struggle with?
3. Did I use cash more than my card?
4. Did I cook at home more than last month?
5. Did I make progress on my debt target?

WEEK 3 CHECK-IN

Use the same set of questions each week:

1. What worked well this week?
2. What did I struggle with?
3. Did I use cash more than my card?
4. Did I cook at home more than last month?
5. Did I make progress on my debt target?

WEEK 4 CHECK-IN

Use the same set of questions each week:

1. What worked well this week?
2. What did I struggle with?
3. Did I use cash more than my card?
4. Did I cook at home more than last month?
5. Did I make progress on my debt target?

MONTH 2 — END-OF-MONTH REFLECTION

1. How much extra did I put toward debt? $______________

2. Did I stay consistent with my savings?

3. Am I feeling more in control?

4. What habit helped me most this month?

5. What slowed me down?

MONTH 3 — GROWTH & CONSISTENCY

This month is about **strength** — staying focused, building momentum, and preparing for long-term success.

MONTH 3 GOALS

1. ______________________
2. ______________________
3. ______________________
4. ______________________

WEEKLY ACTIONS FOR MONTH 3

- Add at least $10–$20 to savings weekly
- Keep following the Eat-In Challenge
- Keep using cash envelopes
- Stay on top of bill due dates
- Track any extra income
- Take one step to grow your hustle

WEEKS 1 CHECK-INS

Use the same questions:

1. Did I save anything this week?
2. Did I stay away from unnecessary spending?
3. What decision helped me the most this week?
4. Did my hustle bring in anything this week?
5. What will I focus on next week?

WEEKS 2 CHECK-INS

Use the same questions:

1. Did I save anything this week?
2. Did I stay away from unnecessary spending?
3. What decision helped me the most this week?
4. Did my hustle bring in anything this week?
5. What will I focus on next week?

WEEKS 3 CHECK-INS

Use the same questions:

1. Did I save anything this week?
2. Did I stay away from unnecessary spending?
3. What decision helped me the most this week?
4. Did my hustle bring in anything this week?
5. What will I focus on next week?

WEEKS 4 CHECK-INS

Use the same questions:

1. Did I save anything this week?
2. Did I stay away from unnecessary spending?
3. What decision helped me the most this week?
4. Did my hustle bring in anything this week?
5. What will I focus on next week?

90-DAY SUMMARY PAGE

Write honestly — you've earned this moment.

INCOME & SAVINGS PROGRESS

- Total saved in 90 days: $__________________
- Debt paid off: $__________________
- New hustle income earned: $__________________

BIGGEST HABIT CHANGES

1.
2.
3.

HOW I FEEL DIFFERENT NOW

WHAT I WILL KEEP DOING FOR THE NEXT 90 DAYS

- ______
- ______
- ______

A MESSAGE TO YOUR FUTURE SELF

Write a short message you can read three months from now:

SECTION 6 — KEEPING YOUR MOMENTUM GOING

You made it through 90 days. Now the goal is to keep going — steady, simple, and consistent. This section shows you how to hold onto your progress and grow it.

6.1 — YOUR NEW MONEY RULES

These rules help you stay in control long-term. Choose the ones that apply to you — and add your own.

MY PERSONAL MONEY RULES

- ☐ Spend with cash first
- ☐ Save before I spend
- ☐ No cruising until my car is paid
- ☐ If I can't pay it in 30 days, I don't need it
- ☐ Eat out only when planned
- ☐ Track every dollar
- ☐ Check accounts twice a week
- ☐ Build my hustle income
- ☐ Keep at least one month of bills saved
- ☐ Stick to my envelopes
- ☐ Pay my bills myself (no auto-drafts)
- ☐ Stay ahead, not behind

Add Your Own Rules:

1. ______________________________
2. ______________________________
3. ______________________________

6.2 — AVOIDING MONEY TRAPS

Money traps are habits that slowly break your progress. Learn to spot them early.

COMMON TRAPS TO WATCH OUT FOR

- ☐ Eating out when stressed
- ☐ Shopping when bored
- ☐ Swiping instead of thinking
- ☐ Borrowing from savings
- ☐ Forgetting to track spending
- ☐ Ignoring bills
- ☐ "I'll start next week"
- ☐ Letting others influence your choices
- ☐ Trying to keep up with friends/family
- ☐ Buying things just for the look

WHICH TRAPS AFFECT YOU MOST?

1. ______________________________
2. ______________________________
3. ______________________________

6.3 — BUILDING A STRONG HUSTLE PLAN

Your hustle is your backup plan and your freedom tool. Here are ways to grow it slowly and safely.

HUSTLE GROWTH QUESTIONS

1. What do I enjoy doing that people ask me for?

 ____

2. What price can I charge consistently?

 ____

3. How many hours a week can I give to my hustle?

 ____

4. What small step can I take this month to grow?

 ____

MONTHLY HUSTLE LOG

Month	Goal	Hours	Money Earned	What Worked	What to Try Next
			$		
			$		
			$		
			$		
			$		
			$		
			$		
			$		
			$		
			$		

6.4 — SAVINGS FOR LIFE

Your savings should keep growing even when life gets busy. This section helps you choose what to save for next.

NEW SAVINGS TARGETS

Choose your next savings goals:

- $1,000 buffer
- 3 months of bills
- Holiday fund
- Car repair fund
- Home repair fund
- New tires / maintenance
- Back-to-school money
- Travel fund
- Emergency healthcare fund

MY NEXT SAVINGS GOALS

1. ________________________________
2. ________________________________
3. ________________________________

SAVINGS CALENDAR SETUP

Month	Goal	Amount Saved	Total
January	______	$______	$______
February	______	$______	$______
March	______	$______	$______
April	______	$______	$______
May	______	$______	$______
June	______	$______	$______
July	______	$______	$______
August	______	$______	$______
September	______	$______	$______
October	______	$______	$______
November	______	$______	$______
December	______	$______	$______

6.5 — WHEN LIFE HAPPENS

Life will happen. Bills pop up... Cars break down... Unexpected things show up... But if you stay steady, nothing can knock you off your plan.

LIFE-HAPPENS PLAN

1. When something unexpected comes up, I will:

   ____

2. Instead of panicking, I will:

   ____

3. My backup plan is:

   ____

4. Someone I can call for wisdom or accountability:

   ____

6.6 — YOUR FINANCIAL FREEDOM PROMISE

Write a simple promise to yourself — something you can keep repeating on tough days.

MY PROMISE

- ★ I promise to stay focused on my financial goals.
- ★ I will spend with purpose, save before I spend, and be honest about my habits.
- ★ I will stay steady even when things get hard.
- ★ My money will work for me — not the other way around.
- ★ I am committed to building a stronger future one day at a time.

Signature ____

Date ______________________________

6.7 — 30-DAY RESTART PLAN

For anytime you fall off track. Even if you slip — you can reset anytime.

RESET STEPS

Week 1: Track everything, switch to cash

Week 2: No eating out

Week 3: Pay on one debt

Week 4: Add to savings

RESET GOALS

1. ______________________________
2. ______________________________
3. ______________________________

APPENDIX — BLANK WORKSHEETS & TEMPLATES

Use these worksheets anytime you want to restart, refresh, or rebuild your financial habits. They are intentionally simple, so they work for all income levels.

A.1 — MONTHLY MONEY SNAPSHOT

Month: ____________________

Income Source	Amount	Notes
____________	$_____	_____
____________	$_____	_____
____________	$_____	_____

Total Monthly Income: $_________________

MONTHLY EXPENSES

Expense	Amount	Paid On	Notes
Rent/Mortgage	$______	______	______
Utilities	$______	______	______
Groceries	$______	______	______
Transportation	$______	______	______
Phone	$______	______	______
Insurance	$______	______	______
Eating Out	$______	______	______
Childcare	$______	______	______
Other	$______	______	______

Total Expenses: $________________

Left Over: $________________

A.2 — DAILY SPENDING LOG

Date	What I Spent On	Amount	Cash or Card?	Notes
______	____________________	$______	☐ Cash ☐ Card	______
______	____________________	$______	☐ Cash ☐ Card	______
______	____________________	$______	☐ Cash ☐ Card	______
______	____________________	$______	☐ Cash ☐ Card	______
______	____________________	$______	☐ Cash ☐ Card	______
______	____________________	$______	☐ Cash ☐ Card	______
______	____________________	$______	☐ Cash ☐ Card	______

A.3 — WEEKLY BUDGET TEMPLATE

Week of: ____________________

Category	**Budget**	**Actual**	**Difference**
Groceries	$______	$______	+/- $______
Gas	$______	$______	+/- $______
Eating Out	$______	$______	+/- $______
Household Items	$______	$______	+/- $______
Personal	$______	$______	+/- $______
Savings	$______	$______	+/- $______
Debt Payment	$______	$______	+/- $______
	$______	$______	+/- $______
	$______	$______	+/- $______

A.4 — CASH ENVELOPE TEMPLATE

Cut out or copy these for physical envelopes.

Envelope Name: ______________________________

Starting Amount: $_________________

Date	Amount Spent	What it Was For	New Balance
______	$______	________________	$______
______	$______	________________	$______
______	$______	________________	$______
______	$______	________________	$______
______	$______	________________	$______
______	$______	________________	$______

A.5 — DEBT TRACKER

Debt Name	Starting Balance	Minimum Payment	Current Balance	Notes
________	$______	$______	$______	______
________	$______	$______	$______	______
________	$______	$______	$______	______
________	$______	$______	$______	______
________	$______	$______	$______	______
________	$______	$______	$______	______
________	$______	$______	$______	______
________	$______	$______	$______	______
________	$______	$______	$______	______
________	$______	$______	$______	______
________	$______	$______	$______	______

A.6 — DEBT SNOWBALL WORKSHEET

List debts from smallest to largest:

Order	Debt	Balance	Minimum Payment
1	______	$______	$______
2	______	$______	$______
3	______	$______	$______
4	______	$______	$______
5	______	$______	$______
6	______	$______	$______
7	______	$______	$______

Extra Payment Amount: $_________________

MONTH-BY-MONTH PROGRESS

Month	Extra Paid	New Balance	Notes
______	$______	$______	______
______	$______	$______	______
______	$______	$______	______
______	$______	$______	______
______	$______	$______	______
______	$______	$______	______
______	$______	$______	______
______	$______	$______	______

______	$______	$______	______
______	$______	$______	______
______	$______	$______	______
______	$______	$______	______

A.7 — SAVINGS GOAL WORKSHEET

Goal Name: ______________________________

Total Needed: $___________________________

Deadline: ________________________________

Break it down:

Timeframe	Amount Needed
Per Month	$______
Per Week	$______
Per Week	$______

Progress Chart:

Deposit Date	Amount Saved	New Total
______	$______	$______
______	$______	$______
______	$______	$______
______	$______	$______

A.8 — EAT-IN TRACKER

Use this to track every time you skip eating out.

Date	**What You Skipped**	**Amount Saved**
______	______	$______
______	______	$______
______	______	$______
______	______	$______
______	______	$______
______	______	$______
______	______	$______
______	______	$______

A.9 — NO-SWIPE CHALLENGE LOG

Day	Swiped? (Yes/No)	Notes
1	☐ Yes ☐ No	______
2	☐ Yes ☐ No	______
3	☐ Yes ☐ No	______
4	☐ Yes ☐ No	______
5	☐ Yes ☐ No	______
6	☐ Yes ☐ No	______
7	☐ Yes ☐ No	______

A.10 — HUSTLE INCOME LOG

Date	What You Did	Hours	Money Earned
______	______	______	$______
______	______	______	$______
______	______	______	$______
______	______	______	$______
______	______	______	$______
______	______	______	$______
______	______	______	$______
______	______	______	$______

A.11 — MONTHLY HUSTLE GOALS

Month: ____________________

1.
2.
3.
4.
5.
6.
7.
8.
9.
10.
11.
12.

WEEKLY CHECK-IN

Week	What Worked	What Didn't	Money Earned	Next Step
1	______	______	$______	______
2	______	______	$______	______
3	______	______	$______	______
4	______	______	$______	______
5	______	______	$______	______

A.12 — BILL PAYMENT SCHEDULE

Use this to avoid late fees and surprises.

Bill	Amount	Due Date	I Will Pay On	Method
______	$______	______	______	Cash/App
______	$______	______	______	Cash/App
______	$______	______	______	Cash/App

A.13 — 30-DAY RESET PLAN

Week 1: Track everything, switch to cash

Week 2: No eating out

Week 3: Pay toward your first debt

Week 4: Add money to savings

RESET GOALS

1. ____________________
2. ____________________
3. ____________________
4. ____________________
5. ____________________
6. ____________________

A.14 — YEARLY OVERVIEW PAGE

(Use to track annual progress.)

SAVINGS

Month	**Amount Saved**
______________________________	$______
______________________________	$______
______________________________	$______
______________________________	$______
______________________________	$______
______________________________	$______
______________________________	$______
______________________________	$______
______________________________	$______
______________________________	$______
______________________________	$______

DEBT

Month	Total Debt
January	$______
February	$______
March	$______
______________________	$______
______________________	$______
______________________	$______
______________________	$______
______________________	$______
______________________	$______
______________________	$______
______________________	$______
______________________	$______

HUSTLE INCOME

Month	Earned
January	$______
February	$______
March	$______
____________________________	$______
____________________________	$______
____________________________	$______
____________________________	$______
____________________________	$______
____________________________	$______
____________________________	$______
____________________________	$______
____________________________	$______

Made in United States
North Haven, CT
04 November 2026

21728938R00077